THE MODERN FABLES OF
HENRY JAMES

THE MODERN FABLES OF
HENRY JAMES

BY

EDWIN MARION SNELL

NEW YORK

Russell & Russell

HARVARD HONORS THESES IN ENGLISH
NUMBER 8

PS
2123
.S6

THE MODERN FABLES OF
HENRY JAMES

THE MODERN FABLES OF HENRY JAMES

THE peculiar quality of Henry James, throughout life, was his detachment. This had something to do with his becoming a writer, and it determined his choice of subject, of attitude, and of method.

He hardly touched and only half understood the people of the great competitive world; the *subject* of his novels was necessarily the leisure class.

His *attitude* toward even this, his own class, was impersonal. He did not share its interests, though he understood them. Besides, he did not share its code. He lived by his own standard: lived to discover the truth of what he saw and to give it palpable form.

This demand for truth and for adequate expression determined the *method* at which he finally arrived. A close observer of society, he made his lifelong study of details only to be able to precipitate the meaning that they held in solution. He tried, in his later novels, to present his achieved logic, not an imitation

[3]

of the chaos with which he as an observer had dealt. He stands, therefore, at the other extreme from the traditional romancer, who by faithfulness to the superficial facts of life obtains consent for his pleasing improbabilities. James belongs with the fabulists, who present impartially their inescapable realities by means of a half-invented world, which we accept because of its consistent, though unliteral reliance on symbols drawn out of the jumbled life from which it is apparently so far removed.

But where the old fabulists spoke for a people and used conventions based on the conditions of common life, James spoke only for himself, necessarily through his own conventions, which were born of his own needs. To criticize the fiction in which he used his unique method, one must know something of his motives and consequent intentions. These I have tried in some measure to explain.

I have tried to analyze (Part I) his early environment as influencing his life, i.e. as confirming his natural detachment, as inducing him to become a writer, and as limiting his choice of material; (Part II) his many experiments as gradually showing him that he could not do his best within the limits of the conventional forms; and (Part III) his approach as finally dictating the peculiar method of his last and best fiction.

I

THE INFLUENCE OF THE BACKGROUND

Henry James's life and work belong to the story of a restless, able family. His grandfather, the elder William James, was born in County Cavan, northern Ireland. According to family tradition he landed in New York in 1789, when he was eighteen.[1] Within four years he had settled in Albany. He died in 1832, a leading citizen of the town, second only to Stephen Van Rensselaer, last of the patroons. His fortune, exceeded by one in the state, that of John Jacob Astor, was estimated at three million dollars.[2]

His seventh child, the elder Henry James, immediately received his share of the fortune, contrary to his father's intention.[3] Having become "leisured for life," he was at a loss for something to do, so after "brief ventures in law and business" he entered Princeton Theological Seminary.[4] By the end of two years, he and his teachers had found him unsuited to the ministry. He left, and married the sister of a fellow in heterodoxy.

The success of the old Albany promoter had freed his descendants from money-grubbing only to impose upon them the choice of a new self-discipline, harder because it had to be undertaken almost without precedent. The United States had offered three sorts of distinction: political, theological, and commercial. Politics was turning into a department of business. Theology was dead: as William the pragmatist was later to remark, "It was anything but a theological age."[5] Business was an endless scramble. Tentative experiments were being made, however, in the direction of secular and unprofessional intellectual distinction, and it was in this new field that the Jameses were to be true pioneers.

The elder Henry James finally turning philosopher and so finding an occupation, became, after his own fashion, a missionary, and of course an unsuccessful one. "A man like my father, lighting on such a time," William was to observe, "is wholly out of his element and atmosphere, and is soon left stranded high and dry." [6] He was not only too much of a mystic but too much of a rebel for the educated class; he was too cosmopolitan and too honest to pose before the populace as a messiah, in that age of messiahs and in a country most avid of them.[7] And though he owed much to Swedenborg and to Fourier, his theology and his philosophy of society remained so completely his own that other followers of those men, among whom he might have hoped for disciples, would never accept him.[8] Received in "blank silence," he nevertheless continued to speak his mind.[9] He found happiness through living whole-heartedly for his ideas, his family, and his friends.

His distrust of existing institutions and current ideology profoundly affected the life of his children. How the Jameses lived and how the children were brought up, we know from *A Small Boy and Others* and *Notes of a Son and Brother*. Austin Warren gives a succinct account of their unusual life:

Tuition the boys had in abundance; but it was scattered and haphazard. Free, by its head's independence of shop and office, to live wherever living seemed at the moment most rich, the family moved restlessly about. If there was a consistency observable in the educational practice of the father, it was suspicion of all consistency, of all system, of all which hardens the individual into the type. . . . His sons were to covet the best gifts, to be *whole men*, not professionals. Detached from trade and from party, from the bigotries of patriotism and religion, they were to cultivate nothing less ample than the universally human.[10]

Henry the elder, in his autobiography, wrote of his own early family surroundings:

I should think, indeed, that our domestic intercourse had been on the whole most innocent as well as happy, were it not for a certain lack of oxygen which is indeed incidental to the family atmosphere, and which I may characterize as the lack of any ideal of action but that of self-preservation.[11]

His attempt to save his own children from this intellectual poverty did not go in vain: Henry the novelist was to have memories far different:

Amid all the Albany issue there was ease, with the habit of ease, thanks to our grandfather's fine old ability — he had decently provided for so large a generation; but our consciousness was positively disfurnished, as that of young Americans went, of the actualities of "business" in a world of business.[12]

To encourage such a state of affairs was, however, to solve but the negative half of the problem. Children's minds must be furnished with something. They were not directly susceptible to the influence of philosophy; "Father's Ideas" were altogether a mystery.[13] What the children did feel was that it was "tasteless and even humiliating that the head of our little family was *not* in business." [14] This was natural:

America was a world so simply constituted that whatever wasn't business or exactly an office or a "store," places in which people sat close and made money, was just simply pleasure, sought, and sought only, in places in which people got tipsy. There was clearly no mean, least of all the golden one, for it was just the ready, even when the moderate, possession of gold that determined, that hurried on, disaster.[15]

The father's constant fear was that his children would be limited to the choice between the countinghouse and the pub.[16]

Only in Europe was there any striking evidence of a possible third course. Henry the elder had no reverence for Europe: "I shouldn't wonder," he wrote to Emerson, "if Barnum grew regenerate in some far-off day by mere force of his democracy."[17] For the present neither Europe nor America was satisfactory: the "far-off day" was conjectural, and Europe's glories were of the past. But those accumulated glories were at least tangibly symbolized; they alone could impress the children with the desirability of something other than business. As early as 1849 the troubled father wrote to Emerson:

considering with much pity our four stout boys, who have no play-room within doors and import shocking bad manners from the street, we gravely ponder whether it wouldn't be better to go abroad for a few years with them, allowing them to absorb French and German and get such a sensuous education as they can't get here.[18]

The family had been once in Europe, in 1844, when Henry was but a year old. This next proposed trip finally came about in 1855, lasted for three years, and was followed by another in the winter of 1859–60.[19]

The trip of 1855 was indeed an event, most of all because it had been so well prepared for. The shadow of Europe had always lived with the Jameses, a presence that Henry was vividly to remember:

> I saw my parents homesick, as I conceived, for the ancient order and distressed and inconvenienced by many of the more immediate features of the modern, as the modern pressed about us, and since their theory of our better living was from an early time that we should renew the quest of the ancient on the very first possibility I simply grew greater in the faith that somehow to manage that would constitute success in life.[20]

It was as a matter of course, then, that he came to look to the European past for a solution of his problems. He was not consciously disloyal in this. It was as an American that he valued the traditions of the older world, the heritage, as he believed, of Americans and Europeans alike. Moreover, he acted neither as philosopher nor as reformer, only as an observer, who had to live by his perceptions and had to make *them* serve for a relationship with the world, in place of that actual membership in a group which he did not find possible.

A Small Boy and Others is filled with references to the early appearance of his peculiar bent, references explained, no doubt colored, by the wise old man of Lamb House, but certainly founded on experience. For example:

What I look back to as my infant license [for wandering about the streets] can only have had for its ground some timely conviction on the part of my elders that the only form of riot or revel ever known to me would be that of the visiting mind.[21]

And American though he was, he felt that Europe promised much more of such indirect experience, which to him was life. In *The American Scene* he reflected:

It was "Europe" that had, in very ancient days, held out to the yearning young American some likelihood of impressions more numerous and various and of a higher intensity than those he might gather on the native scene; and it was doubtless in conformity with some such desire more finely and more frequently to vibrate that he had originally begun to consult the European oracle.[22]

His early letters from abroad, written during his first independent trips, and after 1875, when his emigration had become final, show how large a part Europe had in stimulating and sustaining his powers, though not in "beguiling" or "deluding" him, as Van Wyck

Brooks would have it.[23] Students can but respect this his own so full demonstration of the fact that his decision to leave his own country was not capricious, but necessary and salutary for him. He may well have been thinking partly of himself when he told Howells, "We don't know what people might give us that they don't — the only thing is to take them on what they do and to allow them absolutely and utterly their conditions."[24]

If he was thinking of himself, when he said this, he was thinking especially of his art. His decision to write, like his desire to emigrate, had sprung from his detachment. During the years he spent in America as a young man, his two younger brothers enlisted to fight in the Civil War, and he could not do that on account of an earlier injury.[25] William was already making his way as a brilliant young scientist. Henry felt that he too ought in some way to justify his existence. He was well read and observant: the natural, the almost unavoidable course was to turn man of letters. In this ambition he was confirmed and assisted by C. E. Norton, by E. L. Godkin, editor of the newly founded

Nation, and by W. D. Howells, already assistant editor of the *Atlantic*. They gave him reviewing to do.[26] Howells published his first stories, in which he emulated his two idols, George Eliot and Balzac.[27] But as he made, one after another, honest and futile attempts to write of ordinary Americans, the very detachment that made American life seem thin to him as a man, and had led him to write in the first place, operated to make this life unsatisfactory material for his fiction.

Still, he did not judge unjustly either his country or his own ability. When he was twenty-seven, while he was writing his first novel, the wretched *Watch and Ward*, and was just back from his first independent trip to Europe, he wrote to Norton:

Looking about for myself, I conclude that the face of nature and civilization in this our country is to a certain point a very sufficient literary field. But it will yield its secrets only to a really *grasping* imagination. This I think Howells lacks. (Of course *I* don't!) To write well and worthily of American things one need even more than elsewhere to be a *master*. But unfortunately, one is less![28]

His own country, needing the best prepared of artists, offered the least chance for preparation.[29] Residence in Europe would serve his professional as well as his more purely personal ends. To go abroad to live was not to limit himself in any way. It was only to accept the limitations consequent upon his certain detachment and to act for the best within them.

II

TRIAL AND ERROR

The three earliest stories that James saw fit to include in the definitive New York edition were *A Passionate Pilgrim* (1871), *The Madonna of the Future* (1873), and *Madame de Mauves* (1874.)[30] In the preface to the volume in which they were included he characterized them as "sops instinctively thrown to the international Cerberus formidably posted where I doubtless then didn't quite make him out."[31] His removal to Europe had not shaken his belief in the precedent of the novelists whom he admired, who had written of their own people.[32] But before the American business man, who constituted so much of American life, he was "absolutely and irredeemably helpless," and that was "obviously why, for any decent documentation, I was

[15]

simply shut up to what was left me." [33] What *was* left was the aimless leisure class of Clement Searle, the "passionate pilgrim," who declared, "I should have been born here [in England] and not there [in New York]; here my makeshift distinctions would have found things they'd have been true of."[34] The maturing of James's insight into what was involved in this affirmation was to be the determining fact in his writing.

Since his treatment of American life was to be oblique, since "I was reduced to studying my New Yorkers and my Bostonians . . . under the queer rubric of their more or less stranded helplessness," he could not elude the "international Cerberus," for half his task in describing the American was to show, in juxtaposition, what he was not and what he did not know: Europe was indeed "constantly in requisition as the more salient American stage or more effective *repoussoir*.[35]

His realization that there were advantages to be gained by the further exploitation of this possibility seems to explain the graduated changes in his work between the late sixties, when he was beginning to write of

Americans in Europe, and the very late seventies, when he was turning to a balanced comedy equally involving Europeans and Americans. The earlier stories had involved only the initiation of the American. Of this sort had been *A Passionate Pilgrim*, *Roderick Hudson* (1875), and *The American* (1876–7).[36] Even in the last of these, in which the Bellegardes are a fully developed study of the manners of a "forlorn aristocracy," James ignored the fact that "they would positively have jumped then, the Bellegardes, at my rich and easy American, and not have 'minded' in the least any drawback."[37] He humorously bewailed:

It is difficult for me to-day to believe that I had not, as my work went on, *some* shade of the rueful sense of my affront to verisimilitude; yet I catch the memory at least of no great sharpness, no true critical anguish, of remorse: an anomaly the reason of which in fact now glimmers interestingly out. My concern, as I saw it, was to make and to keep Newman consistent; the picture of his consistency was all my undertaking, and the memory of *that* infatuation perfectly abides with me.[38]

James began, in short, with stories realistic externally and fanciful internally. His passion for essential truth was in the end, however, to make him face about and write stories with a core of observed reality presented through a free, sometimes fanciful rearrangement, in the interest of logic and intensity, of the external facts of life. He was to change from romancer to fabulist.[39]

The first steps in this direction he was already taking: whatever their faults, such stories as *Madame de Mauves* and *The American* represented an advance. In *A Passionate Pilgrim* and *Roderick Hudson* his American protagonists had been influenced principally by the Europe of the Baedeker.[40] Such an experience of European society was too superficial and one-sided to produce important fiction. The narrative gives us only the fact that Americans of leisure are apt to be emotionally starved; all other evaluation has to come through the inadequate device of a *raisonneur*.[41] The advance of the two later stories lay in the attempt to do enough justice to the European side of the story to bring out the character of the Americans. Already James was experimenting toward his famous international comedy of manners (one might almost say, of errors). For, as Edna Kenton declares, "Henry James *was* 'between' countries. There lay his subject and his relation to it, and there was his home."[42]

In *Roderick Hudson* and *The American* he had really wasted two big situations. When he looked back, in the preface to *The Golden Bowl*, "yearning reflection . . . was to reach its maximum . . . over many of the sorry businesses of *The American*."[43] But it had been part of his education. Roderick and Christopher Newman represented the crude archetype to which he was always to be returning, each time with new skill and with added knowledge of what it signified. Roderick and Christopher (and Clement Searle) had the initial qualification of the Jamesian American. They were aware, ruefully, of the lacunae in American life, and so were Americans for whom American life must end in disappointment. Their recounted experiences illustrate, each in its way, James's working hypothesis, that such Americans in Europe should seek but should not find. This was an unreasoned belief: in its interest, as already suggested, he strained plot and character and misinterpreted what he had observed. His failure convinced him, not that he was wrong, but that he had not mastered his evidence and his medium.

So he became the recorder of national types. A half-dozen years after he had published *An International Episode* (1878) he had advanced so far that he could say:

for a Bostonian nymph to reject an English duke is an adventure only less stirring, I should say, than for an English duke to be rejected by a Bostonian nymph. I see dramas within dramas in that, and innumerable points of view.[44]

His longest contribution to this literature of national contrasts was *The Europeans* (1878), of which he wrote to William:

I think I myself estimate the book very justly and am aware of its extreme slightness. . . . I think you are altogether right in returning always to the importance of subject. I hold to this, strongly; and if I don't as yet seem to proceed upon it more, it is because, being "very artistic," I have a constant impulse to try experiments of form, in which I wish not to run the risk of wasting or gratuitously using big situations. But to these I am coming now. It is something to know how to write, and when I look round me and see how few people (doing my sort of work) know how (to my sense,) I don't regret my step-by-step evolution.[45]

Washington Square and *The Portrait of a Lady*, both begun in 1879, mark his first return to the big situation. The one deals with an exclusively American aspect: its central character is too unimaginative ever to try the European alternative. Since James was not often to follow it up and did not include it in the definitive edition, it has been considered an aberration, on the assumption that he could write naturally only in one style.[46] In reality, the almost simultaneous production of two such novels, so dissimilar in treatment, is proof that he developed his style to suit what he had to say.

What he was saying in *Washington Square* was just what he was neglecting to say in *The Portrait of a Lady*. Catherine Sloper and Isabel Archer are both American girls who become rich; there the resemblance ends. Catherine, as her embittered father mentally comments, is 'decidedly not brilliant.'[47] Her one experience, an unfortunate love affair, is so handled by her father and worthless lover that she has no chance to do anything positive, and her one significant feeling is the numb pain of frustration. James borrowed the plot from his admired Balzac's *Eugénie Grandet*, but the substance of the story was his own, and American. The thinness of that New York life of his boyhood, the background of the story, made him, as he told Howells, feel the virtual impossibility of there ever being an American Balzac, a great annalist of urban American life, at least during his lifetime.[48] He had to make that thinness into a positive value, and he carried it off remarkably well, nowhere better than in the last scene. Eugénie and Charles Grandet had, after all, lived; James turned to his expert use the fact that Catherine Sloper and Morris Townshend could only become desolate.

Going on to *The Portrait of a Lady* we remember that Catherine Sloper spent a year in Europe without in any way responding. Isabel Archer, the "lady," *en devint fou*. Discussing in the preface how this novel came to be, James appealed to the precedent of Turgenieff, for whom also a story began "with the vision of some person or persons who hovered before him . . . appealing to him just as they were and by what they were."[49] If the inspiration of *Washington Square* had been the figure of Catherine Sloper, the background still seemed significant enough to impel James to break with Balzac and to

indicate, in the title, that his interest was
more in the situation than in the heroine.
The Portrait of a Lady had grown out of
the necessity felt by him of giving Isabel,
with all her desire and ability and opportunity for experience, a chance to live.
Fresh from Albany, she embraces the
chance, yet her fate were scarcely better
than Catherine's did she not choose it,
freely, held back by no desire for life on
easy terms. The delusion practiced upon
her is cruel indeed, and her contrasted high
bravery but intensifies James's new picture
of the disillusionment awaiting eager, quix-
otic, ignorant Americans.[50] A "lady" she
is called in the title, and if sympathetically,
no less ironically.

Catherine, unintelligent, coerced, had en-
dured life; Isabel, intelligent, free, had
sought it. Only through characters of the
second sort, and through actions suited to
them, could James develop as a novelist. The
leisure class that he described was not
enough subject to the blind uncertainties,
nor enough mixed up in the bitter competi-
tion of Balzac's world; what observably
happened to it was scant material for fiction.

But its measure of its own quiet affairs offered many possibilities, for it became James's settled belief, as he was to give it the preface to *The Princess Casamassima*, in that "experience, as I see it, is our apprehension and our measure of what happens to us as social creatures," that is, our coming to realize where we stand.[51] His novels were inevitably stories of orientation, variations on one motif: that of an individual's coming to comprehend, through some situation, his real position in industrialized society. Such experience James understood from his own life.

The first great theme of his, that of the American in Europe, had been only a phase of that larger theme, though a most significant one. And in the three novels that succeeded *The Portrait of a Lady*: *The Bostonians* and *The Princess Casamassima* (both of 1885) and *The Tragic Muse* (1890), he turned from the purely international aspect in order to give an account of possible relationships in other frames of reference.

The Princess Casamassima was first the fascinating Christina Light of *Roderick Hudson*, the illegitimate daughter of an

American dowager and an Italian *cavaliere*. At the end of *Roderick Hudson*, after she has been bullied into marrying an admirable, dull, stubborn Italian prince, we get a last glimpse of her, leading herself and her husband a restless life satisfying to neither of them. At the beginning of the novel that bears her name she has already been separated from the Prince and has formed connections with a revolutionary group. About it we know only that its headquarters are in Germany and that it has plans. This vagueness was intentional: James wanted to describe such a movement as seen from without; the idea for the novel had, indeed, come from his walking the streets of "the great gray Babylon" London, and from his wondering, then, what was going on among the inarticulate masses.[52]   In the Princess, dissatisfaction with social routine we meet merely a new aspect of the satiety felt by bourgeois who have been assimilated into the aristocracy. The Princess, somewhat naively and as a woman, is trying to exchange what she feels to be the pointlessness of her adopted life for an illusion of purpose: "She would be world-weary — that was

another of her notes."[53] And James did very
well by her, without writing a strong, or even
coherent novel.

The Bostonians has the faults and few of
the redeeming qualities of *The Princess Casamassima*. It takes in several phases of
nineteenth-century urban American life,
and is focused, of course, on the ineffectual
life of people of leisure. Basil Ransom is one
of the southern planters who have moved
north, after the war, to become half-hearted
second-rate lawyers. The group centering
on Olive Chancellor represents the final de-
generation of the humanitarian tradition of
New England. Mrs. Burrage and Mrs. Luna
are well-to-do New Yorkers of the new sort,
who entertain themselves by "taking up"
people.

The Tragic Muse, also striving for quantitative adequacy, contrasts different careers
by means of a group of English people. It is
another commentary on the life of the upper
classes. This had become James's main subject, and national characteristics had become, for him, only the incidental variations
which provided material for drama. *The
Tragic Muse* is not unsuccessful, only undis-

tinguished. When James had finished it, he described it as "void and dead."[54]

He had reached the end of that "only period in which his heroes and heroines are really up to anything in particular, have professions, missions, practical aims."[55] For ten years he had tried to describe the upper classes as such through their activities — and the result did not satisfy him. The conventional novel-form had failed him, or he had failed it. He had begun, thinking he knew how to write, yet he must be wrong: his ambitious quantitative analyses had achieved, not lucidity, only a disappointing diffuseness. The novelist who in 1878 had eagerly looked forward to writing of "big situations" said, in 1890, of *The Tragic Muse*, "[it] is to be my last long novel."[56]

He had always thought of writing for the stage. "Happy man," he told Howells in 1880, "to be going, like that, to see your plays acted. It is a sensation I am dying (though not as yet trying) to cultivate."[57] To William he had confided, less than two years earlier, "it has long been my most earnest and definite intention to commence at play-writing as soon as I can."[58] That the

theater had always had a special attraction
for him is clear from *A Small Boy and Others*,
where so many of his memories are connected
with performances which he had seen while
very young, in New York, London, and
Paris. His detailed study of the French
theater is attested by his essay on it in
French Poets and Novelists. His long corre-
spondence with Elizabeth Robins, beginning
early in the nineties and continuing to the
end of his life, contains abundant evidence
of his concern with every sort of drama, and
especially with the fate of the English
theater.[59] This very subject, finally, is discussed at some length in *The Tragic Muse*.

Yet, up to 1890, he had not acted on this
long felt interest. What led him, for five
years, to write plays was his disappointment
with his last novels. If, after all, he was not
able to grapple with *subject*, if he must go
back, learn more about technique, develop
a new approach, the dramatic form with its
wonderful lucidity was unquestionably the
one to cultivate. And what could be more
pleasant than to indulge, together, his old
love of the theater and his need for more
skill in writing? So, in 1890, he had set

his task and was saying, "I shall never make my fortune — nor anything like it; but — I know what I shall do, and it won't be bad."[60] He was to practise writing, in a form worth studying — and he hoped to make the practice pay for itself. The venture was "not to depend on a single attempt, but on half a dozen of the most resolute and scientific character." [61]

Altogether, he wrote eight plays.[62] Two of them did reach the stage, but even those two did not please the public. As early as 1894, when the final blow was yet to come, he was wiser by a great deal, wise enough to exclaim, "I may have been meant for the Drama — God knows! — but I certainly wasn't meant for the Theatre."[63] His friends had been begging him to give up. But only when *Guy Domville* was unfavorably received by a London audience early in 1895 did he decide to make no further attempt to be a playwright.[64] A French audience might applaud his deft fulfilment of the conditions of the stage, and the more able English critics did approve, but the London audience preferred Oscar Wilde.[65]

He quickly got over the "ordeal" at the

St. James Theatre on the occasion of the opening of *Guy Domville*, swallowed his disappointment, and at once found himself, not downcast but elated.[66] Less than a week after the incident he wrote to William: "But I am not plangent — one must take the thick with the thin — and I have such possibilities of another and better sort before me."[67] Only two weeks later he wrote to Howells, "I have, potentially, improved immensely, and am bursting with ideas and subjects."[68]

His five years' unpleasant connection with the London theater has often been deplored.[69] To such maudlin superstition his preface to *Theatricals, Second Series* (1895), which contains two of his unacted plays, is the best reply:

> The constant pursuit of it [success as a playwright] comprehends, I think, more private generalisations, more stores of technical experience, than any other aesthetic errand; and these secret hoards may not unreasonably be expected to supply, sooner or later, in most cases, the ringing metal with which the adventurer shall pay his way.[70]

III

THE ACHIEVED METHOD AND FORM

James had at last found a method suited to his impersonal interest in the psychological processes of his class. At last he could afford to dispense with the clumsy methods of the conventional novelist, methods with which he had made endless experiment. All the fiction he was to write thereafter was to bear the stamp of his knowledge of and admiration for the dramatic technique. "I mean," he explained near the end of his career, "I come back, I come back yet again and again, to my only seeing it in the dramatic way — as I can only see everything and anything now.[71] All his mature writings on the art of fiction include some expression of this belief.[72] His work from 1895 on, Francis Fergusson calls "drama without a stage."[73] Yet he did not compose plays to be read as plays, to be imagined as being acted on a stage; he presented, instead, stage, costumes, gestures — everything — on the printed page along with the mere lines. And this work satisfied him.

[31]

That he intended it to be artificial and gloried in its formal perfection is only too apparent, but it was because he held that meaning *could* not exist apart from its presentation.[74] His conventions were eccentric (Ezra Pound has classed him as one of the true innovators) because he found no accepted conventions at hand adaptable to his specialized meaning. He did not cultivate technique for its own sake. Few understood this so well as his good friend Joseph Conrad, who wrote to Galsworthy, in 1899:

Technical perfection, unless there is some real glow to illumine and warm it from within, must necessarily be cold. I argue that in H. J. there is such a glow and not a dim one either, but to us used, absolutely accustomed, to unartistic expression of fine, headlong, honest (or dishonest) sentiments the art of H. J. does appear heartless. The outlines are so clear, the figures so finished, chiselled, carved and brought out that we exclaim, — we, used to the shades of the contemporary fiction, to the more or less malformed shades, — we exclaim, — stone! Not at all. I say flesh and blood, — very perfectly presented, — perhaps with too much perfection of *method*.[75]

The Spoils of Poynton (1896) was James's first novel in his "later manner." It came from a "casual hint . . . dropped unwittingly by my neighbor [at dinner], a mere floating particle in the stream of talk." This was enough. "There had been but ten words, yet I had recognized in them, as in a flash, all the possibilities of the little drama of my *Spoils*." But as the neighbor went on talking James "saw clumsy Life again at her stupid work," and for all the rest of her story he "had absolutely and could have, no scrap of use."[76]

These remarks point to James's growing obsession, a desire for moral lucidity, rather than for literal faithfulness to life. He was no student of sociology, economics, history. All his perceptions were immediate. Those miscellaneous works of his in which he described society first lead one to believe that this immediate perception was confined to the aesthetic aspect, but one sees, on looking more carefully, that aesthetic facts, far from being final, always meant, for him, the ends for which some group had lived or was living.[77] Faced with Balzac and the French naturalists, he willingly conceded the great workability of the sordid elements in life. But he was, for his time, preternaturally aware of the real fallacy behind many of the romantic

attempts of even the most honest realistic
novelists. Art was by nature selection, limi-
tation, which flourished not by competing
with life in the gross, but by extracting faith-
fully its essence.[78] He said in the preface to
Roderick Hudson:

> Really, universally, relations stop nowhere,
> and the exquisite problem of the artist is eternally
> but to draw, by a geometry of his own, the circle
> within which they shall happily *appear* to do so.[79]

Encyclopedic inclusiveness was surely a delusion. The artist's goal was convincingly to
describe what seemed essential: the moral
values, which could best be summarized in
the choices of those free to choose, and in the
judgments of those able to think. To make
them bear the full weight of their responsibility, the artist must draw his circle so as to
exclude the "fatuity of fact;" the logic of the
development of his story must be complete,
must flow from relationships sought or accepted at the outset. "Clumsy Life" did not
operate thus, even among James's friends,
but the great artists had so operated. And if
life only offered the hint, the artist doing the
rest, one's observation, no matter how limited, was quite enough to start from. As

James declared in the preface to *Lady Barbarina*:

> The great truth in the whole connexion . . . is, I think, that one never really chooses one's general range of vision — the experience from which ideas and themes and suggestions spring: this proves ever what it has *had* to be. . . . The artist — for it is of this strange brood we speak — has but to have his honest sense of life to find it fed at every pore even as the birds of the air are fed.[80]

From 1896 to 1904 he published eight novels. The first five: *The Spoils of Poynton* (1896), *The Other House* (1896), *What Maisie Knew* (1897), *The Awkward Age* (1898–9), and *The Sacred Fount* (1901), were short and of a specially marked dramatic character. His last complete novel, *The Outcry*, was a belated member of this group, originating in 1909 as a play requested, though never used, by an ephemeral London repertory company.[81] Longer and of a much fuller development were *The Wings of the Dove* (1902), *The Ambassadors* (1903), and *The Golden Bowl* (1904). *The Ivory Tower* and *The Sense of the Past*, his two unfinished novels, published in 1917 after his death, were also of this sort.

In the more compact stories resembling

[35]

plays, all published by 1901 (except *The Outcry*) he restricted himself to a logically complete demonstration of his subject, eliminating, like a playwright, every aspect of character and incident that did not seem necessary to the logic. Even then they outgrew his original intentions.[82]

These novels all dealt with the British leisure class, about which he was always, in private, most out-spoken, as for instance, with reference to "the hideous — divorce case, which will besmirch exceedingly the already very damaged prestige of the English upper class":

> The condition of that body seems to me to be in many ways like that of the French aristocracy before the revolution — minus cleverness and conversation; or perhaps it's more like the heavy, congested and depraved Roman world upon which the barbarians came down.[83]

But because he was an artist, he saw what the partisan novelist will rarely admit: that the state of a social group is not to be shown by the proportion of good or bad people in it (a proportion perhaps almost constant), but by the sort of life forced upon good and bad alike by virtue of their membership. He also realized that the merit of fiction depends no more on the effect of environment on character than on the response of character to environment. The latter, in fact, was the real issue.

Dealing with subject as measured by characters involved, he used their measure not as a static or a merely contributory element, but as a *process and a primary force itself constituting the real action.* The great technical problem, involving a host of lesser ones, was this: the reader's degree of enlightenment must always be just enough greater than that possessed by any of the characters, to allow him to grasp the immediate significance of the difference between what each of them does know and what he does not know; yet it must never become great enough to destroy his interest in the gradual clarification of issues going on before him. For that reason he must *see* what is happening; it must never (in theory) be outlined or explained — hence James's extension, into the smallest detail, of the technique of the dramatist.

The actual procedure varies, of course, from book to book. In *What Maisie Knew* there is one central recorder, a little girl each of whose parents has formed another relationship. James managed uncannily to convey all the implications of the theme without going outside the account given by naive, if precocious Maisie. His dramatic irony is perfect. In *The Sacred Fount*, on the other hand, the truth of the recording is more difficult to estimate. It is done by an adult male who makes a nuisance of himself on a week-end party in the country by prying into the sexual relationships among his fellow-guests. This in itself may not be remarkable, but it is strange that he seems unable to understand what he sees; his whole hypothesis of the "sacred fount" is a misinterpretation of it. We are told no more about him than about Maisie, and he cannot so easily be placed, but it seems probable that he was conceived as an objective study in the mentality of homosexuality.[84] *The Awkward Age* is concerned with what happens when an adolescent girl becomes old enough to *assist* at her mother's salon, where the conversation is, to use James's word, "good." Several of the main characters take turns in recording this half-profound and wholly discomfiting story of modern morals.

If James, in accordance with the tradition of English fiction, had only appeared in these novels himself, as the omniscient and critical author, they would have been not only easier to read, but less disquieting. But he was resolved to be only the showman, presenting his actions without comment, letting the reader see for himself, as the story progresses, the abyss between what the characters know at first and what they learn, between what they know and what they do not, and above all, between cultivated appearances and the corresponding reality.[85] The irony thus achieved should grow on him with his every rereading. On this aspect of James's book Theodora Bosanquet, long his secretary, comments acutely, remarking, among other things, that "between the people created by Henry James lying is as frequent as among mortals and not any easier to detect."[86] Why must James's readers, seeing the vacuity of the life he described ("highly modern and 'actual,'" as he said), incautiously deny that he saw it, disregard his ironic detachment, read him into all his characters, make him plead for them? This is to ignore the significance of his technique. And why must they insist on treating his fables as if they were meant to be a literal transcript of "reality," a *tranche de vie*, when they deal only with realities abstracted, formalized, rearranged?[87]

The novels we have just considered, called "technical exercises" by Beach, were suggested by relationships, that is, by character as illustrating and as illustrated by a particular situation. They were not, like his earlier and later *novels*, inspired by complete characters *in vacuo*, appealing to have something done with them. There was no lack of subject, but it was not illuminated by the presence of figures conceived as having past and future; the illusion of artistic completeness is so thorough as to deprive one of the imaginative resource so important in the appreciation of the best fiction and drama: the feeling that the characters are great enough to include the possibilities of many other equally meaningful adventures.

The presence of this resource is what distinguishes James's latest and finest novels: *The Wings of the Dove*, *The Ambassadors*, and *The Golden Bowl*, and those two admirable fragments, *The Ivory Tower* and *The Sense of the Past*. Their length, and the reintroduction of Americans, are not signs of a change in technique or in subject, only of a renewed desire once more to do full justice to his characters. He felt himself absolute master of his medium, able to come back, for the second time, to his first great theme, into the presentation of which he now easily poured all his accumulated wisdom. He used the opposition of America to Europe, not for itself, of course, but to show the real identity in the position of the leisure classes of both continents. And this demonstration itself existed to the end of portraying the entangled human beings.

The theme was the old one. Americans of leisure, ill at ease at home, yearned to be sanctified by, and absorbed into, an organism which had paraphernalia and code and history, not realizing at first that they were admiring mere vestiges of an order once but no longer functional, and thus were only exchanging unorganized for organized uselessness. Their European friends, accepting them, realistically, for their money and vigor, succeeded, for a while, in hiding their own bad faith. But it was only a matter of time before the Americans saw that they *had* bought a shadow, that they were cultivating a ritual satisfactory only to its hereditary exponents. The ordeal of the frustrate Americans, coming at the climax, was to face the fact of their homelessness, and to make the best of the situation. And their decisions involved more than the choice between two continents.

It is easy to see how well this sort of story fell in with James's already developed technique. His Europeans are anxious to protect his Americans, to keep them from understanding. The Americans, as they begin to understand, try to keep the Europeans, and even one another, from the disturbing knowledge that they do understand. The whole theme is perfectly adapted to the dramatic method of gradual revelation and ironic, if sympathetic contrast.

In *The Golden Bowl* Maggie Verver, a rich American, buys herself an Italian prince and then, to keep her father, also a collector of rarities, from becoming lonely, marries him off to her old friend Charlotte Stant, an American expatriate. Neither Maggie nor her father knows that the Prince was once Charlotte's lover (they were too poor to get married). Charlotte and the Prince soon find their newly established propinquity (and the unremedied ignorance of their respective *sposi*) too great a temptation. Their infidelity is discovered by Maggie and by her father, independently; but neither reveals his knowledge, for fear of injuring the other or of estranging one or both of the purchased mates. The last half of the novel is a minute account of the way in which Maggie becomes certain and, without speaking out or making a scene, forces her husband and stepmother to terms. This book well illustrates James's talent for vivid presentation (not explanation) of successive psychological states. The accumulated intensity is held in reserve till the very end, when it all helps to give force to Maggie's final momentous actions.

The Ambassadors is well enough known to need no summary; here it is necessary only to point out that Lambert Strether, the first ambassador commissioned by his New England patroness to bring back her expatriate son, has lost, by the end of the story, even the satisfaction of believing that had he lived in Europe, he would really have lived. He begins by discovering how much Europe,

in the person of Mme. de Vionnet, has done
for Chad Newsome, and ends by finding how
little it has done. The novel, after preparing
for his first discovery, describes the process
by which he arrives at the second. "Live all
you can," he has told Little Bilham on that
crucial mild Sunday afternoon in Gloriani's
garden; "it's a mistake not to. . . . One has
the illusion of freedom; therefore don't be,
like me, without the memory of that illusion."[88] But by the end, though he does not
renounce this opinion, he has lost the inno-
cence that made it all so simple.[89] He has
discovered and has accepted the fact that he
was really doomed, from the beginning, to
have no part to play in life, even with the
help of Europe. *The Ambassadors* is without
question James's most perfect treatment of
all that he saw as involved in the dilemma of
the American in Europe, and of the man of
leisure in the industrialized world.

The Wings of the Dove is a sinister affair,
from beginning to end skilfully pressing but
never hammering the note of sordidness. Yet
the reader of this novel, as of any of the
others, does well to be circumspect in the
matter of deciding what was James's attitude

toward the characters. All, and it is little yet more than enough, that keeps Kate Croy and Merton Densher from being decent is their upper middle class belief in the supreme importance of money. Merton is himself corrupted by Kate, to whom and to whose background we are introduced in the very first scene. Obviously to her disadvantage, James played her off against Milly Theale, the consumptive New York heiress. Yet it seems unlikely that the commentators, who have seen this much, have got quite to the bottom of James's irony. Millie, who comes to a muffled end in far-off Venice, does undoubtedly win out, by a fine generosity born of knowledge, but the final irony is reserved for Kate, in London. For Kate, all helpless, looked-for success is turned to ashes, because of her opponent's very generosity, on which she has counted without foreseeing all its effects. Kate has had to fight her own way as she could, for the ends and with the means of her own class. Who of us, after all, will throw the first stone? Not, to be sure, Henry James.[90]

If one doubt his statement that in his later novels he was never dealing with national types merely as such, one need only turn to *The Ivory Tower*, in which, at last enabled to treat American life (or at least a little of it), he described what some have thought him to regard as typically European frailties.[91] When the story opens, in the quiet Newport autumn, the wise self-made millionaire, Mr. Betterman, is dying (much to the interest of a former partner, who once defrauded him, and is now kept alive only by his curiosity to learn how much Betterman is now worth). Betterman, as his parting jest, leaves his money to an unworldly nephew, Graham Fielder, who has been living in Europe: leaves it to him, as he says, just because he is unworldly, because what will happen to him will be an interesting experiment. Graham's numerous (of course) friends at Newport are all "wonderful" to him. He entrusts his money to one of the most wonderful, "Haughty" Vint, a relatively poor young man who (again) is not getting married because he could not carry it off in the proper, the Newport style. James did not finish the story, but his notes make it clear that the temptation of being utterly trusted will be too much for "Haughty." Finished,

The Ivory Tower might have proved James's masterpiece.[92]

Like Thomas Gray, to whom A. C. Benson compared him, Henry James "never spoke out."[93] His medium was formalized, his manner oblique; we cannot hastily come to what he is saying. Besides, he was objective; what he gives us is observation, never dogma.

Had not the one problem of his background been that of the leisure class, had he not, because of that very background, felt incompetent to describe the American business man, he might have followed up his numerous tentative imitations of Hawthorne, Balzac, and George Eliot, might have become a skilful local-color novelist. As it was, he saw above all the helplessness of similarly placed compatriots, saw in their struggles — and, for that matter, in his own and those of his family — the urge toward assimilation into the apparently satisfied leisure class of the old world. He saw, he himself went through, early in life, their inevitable disillusionment. But how to record it?

He found his answer, after many years of slow experiment, in the psychological drama

[47]

of his last novels. On the surface he could present all the charm of the old world; underneath, the spiritual tortuosities of his frustrate characters — without interfering himself, without breaking the spell.

The result was conventional, though not traditional. To formal art as such, most serious readers do not object. Indeed, from ancient times through the Renaissance art was expected to be conventional, and its conventions were understood. But the modern world has changed too rapidly and too often to allow for the accumulation of convention. The modern form *par excellence*, the novel, has been altogether loose and explicit; it has, in the main, expressed the easiest things in the easiest way. If James were not to do violence to his sensitive observation, he came to believe that he must invent his form and resign himself to its being generally misunderstood. He still hoped, of course, for some attention. The prefaces to the New York edition were one long exhortation to him who would listen, asking that he participate actively when reading. "They are, in general," he told Howells, "a sort of plea for

Criticism, for Discrimination, for Appreciation on other than infantile lines. . . ."[94]

Even those who have heeded this petition have criticized James's objectivity on another ground: he has no dogma, and "we would have a sign." "Thank God," he wrote in 1898, to one of his nephews, "Thank God I've no *opinions* — not even on the Dreyfus case."[95] According to Elizabeth Robins, who knew him intimately for many years, he had ever "the look of silent inward laughter, a laughter never with safety to be interpreted as with, but *at* something or somebody, probably the one nearest."[96] Who was he to dogmatize? It was true that the leisure class had no function, and therefore neither ethic nor occupation. But James had nothing to offer. He was content to perceive, and from his perceptions to create art as final as possible, fables containing few grudges and as few illusions. Thus he escaped the ephemeral theorizings that have already begun to invalidate the work of Hardy, Shaw, Wells, D. H. Lawrence. His individualism was, in its way, no less wasteful than theirs: he had always to experiment and to throw away, to write little that was his best, that painfully, and for very few. It is idle to ask whether he should have "joined up," should have spoken for a group. He knew what he could do, he knew 'it wouldn't be bad.' For that one must respect him, particularly today.

NOTES

1. See H. A. Larrabee, "The Jameses: Financier, Heretic, Philosopher," *The American Scholar*, I (1932), 401–413. 401–402.
2. For the life of the elder William James see Larrabee; also Austin Warren, *The Elder Henry James*, New York, 1934, 2 ff.
3. The elder William James had, in his will, provided that "in view . . . of the lamentable consequences which so frequently result to young persons brought up in affluence from coming at once into the possession of property," his estate should not be settled "until the youngest of my children and grandchildren living at the date of this my will and attaining the age of twenty-one years shall have attained that age." Furthermore, in order to qualify as beneficiaries, three of his sons and a grandson "must severally learn some one of the professions, trades or occupations usually pursued in this country as a livelihood, and must assiduously pursue and practice the same." Warren, 3–4. Two of his sons, the elder Henry James and another, were cut off with small annuities, on account of theological differences with their father (Larrabee, 409–410). The probate court did not, however, allow the will, and assigned equal shares in the estate to the widow and each of the children. See Warren, 21.
4. For these and the succeeding facts about the life of the elder Henry James, see Warren, especially 21 ff., 34, 38.

5. *The Literary Remains of the Late Henry James*, ed. William James, Boston, 1884, 119.

6. *Ibid.*

7. The elder Henry James's "moralistic and radical views of the economic and social order were fortified and sharpened by his association, from 1847 on, with that remarkable group of disciples of the French socialist Fourier which had gathered in New York city. . . . But his Fourierism, like his Sandemanianism and Swedenborgianism, was not an affair of institutionalized overt action, but a conviction held 'in his own peculiar way;' so that he continued all his life long to derive from the inheritance left by his ultra-orthodox father the income which supported his heretical writings" (Larrabee, 411–412).

8. "His [the elder Henry James's] piety, which sometimes expressed itself in terms of alarming originality and freedom, was too large for any ecclesiastical limits, and one may learn from the books which record it how absolutely individual his interpretations of Swedenborg were. Clarification they cannot be called, and in that other world whose substantial verity was the inspiration of his life here, the two sages may by this time have met and agreed to differ as to some points in the doctrine of the Seer. In such a case, I cannot imagine the apostle giving way; and I do not say he would be wrong to insist, but I think he might now be willing to allow that the exegitic pages which sentence by sentence were so brilliantly suggestive, had sometimes

a collective opacity which even the most resolute vision could not penetrate" (William Dean Howells, *Literary Friends and Acquaintances*, New York, 1901, 266).

9. See Warren, 168, also Larrabee, 410.

10. Warren, 127–128. See *A Small Boy and Others*, New York, 1913, especially 16 ff.

11. *Literary Remains*, 152. The quotation is from "Immortal Life," ed. Henry James. On the word of William James we may take this to be his father's autobiography, attributed to "an entirely fictitious personage" in accordance with his belief that the differences between men were vain and inconsequential, and should not be emphasized. See *ibid.*, 7. "Nothing so endlessly besotted in Mr. James's eyes as the pretension to possess personally any substantive merit or advantage whatever" (*ibid.*, 75). Also, see Warren, 227–228.

12. *A Small Boy and Others*, 57.

13. *Notes of a Son and Brother*, New York, 1914, 155 ff.; see also Warren, 151.

14. *Ibid.*, 68.

15. *A Small Boy and Others*, 49.

16. "The grim little generalisation remained, none the less, and I may speak of it — since I speak of everything — as still standing: the striking evidence that scarce aught but disaster *could*, in that so unformed and unseasoned society, overtake young men who were in the least exposed. Not to have been immediately launched in business of a rigorous sort was to *be* exposed — in the absence I mean of some fairly abnormal predisposi-

tion to virtue" (*ibid.*, 48–49). His grandfather's will had indeed been prophetic, had been drawn up with great good sense. See above, note 3.

17. *Notes of a Son and Brother*, 207. The elder James once told Godkin, editor of the *Nation*, that a crowded Cambridge horsecar 'was the nearest approach to Heaven on earth.' Warren, 185.

18. *Notes of a Son and Brother*, 195–196.

19. *The Letters of Henry James*, ed. Percy Lubbock, New York, 1920; from the first of several biographical sketches, "First European Years," I, 1–14.

20. *A Small Boy and Others*, 84. James recalled his parents' conversation: "Had *all* their talk for its subject, in my infant ears, that happy time? — did it deal only with London and Picadilly and the Green Park?" (p. 82.)

21. *A Small Boy and Others*, 25. See also *ibid.*, 288.

22. *The American Scene*, London, 1907, 365. The superiority of Europe for his purposes is demonstrated by this very book, the outcome of a short trip back to America in 1904, when he had been absent for more than twenty years, and had made his home in Europe for almost thirty. Its eminence (in spite of Bliss Perry's patronizing verdict, it is one of the finest books ever written of our country) carries with it an irony perhaps unique. James stated it politely in the preface: "My cultivated sense of aspects and prospects affected me absolutely as an enrichment of my subject" (*ibid.*, vi). Mr. Perry

speaks of James as "avoiding his native country for nearly thirty years and then returning for a few months to write that *American Scene* which he understood far less truly than any immigrant" (*Commemorative Tribute to Henry James*, American Academy of Arts and Letters, 1922, 2). For an antidote to this "tribute" see Ezra Pound, in *Instigations*, New York, 1920, also Lawrence Leighton, "Armor Against Time," *Hound & Horn*, VII (April–June, 1934), 382–383.

23. For the close observation of significant social phenomena, even American social phenomena, Europe offered James the best training, as he thought. See, for his dissatisfaction with America, *The American Scene*, 367–368. James's earlier letters indicate how stimulating, on the other hand, he found Europe (see *Letters*, I, 19–20, 24, 48, 74–75).

VanWyck Brooks, in *The Pilgrimage of Henry James*, quotes or paraphrases many such letters, but he takes them to mean that James went abroad full of romantic illusions, which, later on, he lost. "Decidedly England [at about 1910] had not lived up to his expectations. Yes, he had been beguiled, he had been deluded" (*The Pilgrimage of Henry James*, New York, 1925, 148). To say this is altogether to ignore the fact that James went abroad on "the quest of the ancient," on the search for inspiration from the precedent established in the old world through many centuries, but that he did not on that account have to be beguiled by the Europe of his own day. It was the "modern" that "pressed about" him and his family, America merely standing for the unmitigated modern. That he saw the faults of the leisure classes of both continents, from the beginning of his expatriation, is shown in many letters (see *Letters*, I, 19, 22, 23, 26–27, 28, 37, 51, 58, 63, 68, 69, 72, 113–114, 124, 126, 143, 155 — these summarize his opinions down to 1890).

Moreover, in *A Passionate Pilgrim* (1871), the earliest story of James's to be retained for the definitive New York edition, his point of view is perfectly established, though it has usually been misinterpreted. The first-person narrator, obviously James himself, is a disillusioned, if sympathetic young man, *speaking of* the slight adventures of Clement Searle, an aging New Yorker full of illusions. The narrator (James) is no "passionate pilgrim." For a thorough discussion of the repeated misunderstandings on the part of critics, and for an excellent analysis of the story, see Cornelia Pulsifer Kelley, *The Early Development of Henry James*, Urbana, Illinois, 1930, particularly 117 ff.

24. *Letters*, I, 164. At another time James remarked, "Meanwhile, I repeat, we do not judge the artist with fairness unless we say to him, 'Oh, I grant you your starting-point, because if I did not I should seem to prescribe to you, and heaven forbid I should take that responsibility" ("The Art of Fiction," *Partial Portraits*, London, 1888, 396). "The Art of Fiction" was originally published in *Longman's*, December, 1884.

25. James once discussed the injury which made him unfit for any strenuous physical activity. "Jammed into the acute angle between two high fences," he said, in explaining the incident, "where the rhythmic play of my arms, in tune with that of several pairs, but at a dire disadvantage of position, induced a rural, a rusty, a quasi-extemporised old engine to work and a saving stream to flow, I had done myself, in face of a shabby conflagration, a horrid even if an obscure hurt" (*Notes of a Son and Brother*, 297–298). See also *ibid.*, 241. It was probably hernia; according to Percy Lubbock it was "an accidental strain." *Letters*, I, 9. At any rate, it made him feel very much out of things, and also "gave him many years of uncertain health" (*ibid.*).

26. "The first review appeared in October, 1864; seventeen reviews and a short story followed during the next year; twelve reviews and two stories the next, and so on in varying ratio, increasing rapidly during the seventies with notes on art, on travel, on the theatre running the reviews a close race while the original fiction often trailed far in the rear" (Kelley, 13). Miss Kelley discusses them ably, at length; Morris Roberts, in *Henry James's Criticism*, Cambridge, Mass., 1929, Chapter I, deals with them more briefly, with apt quotations. For published collections of the reviews see the Bibliography, under James's miscellaneous work.

27. See J. W. Beach, *The Method of Henry James*, New Haven, 1918, 165–190, and,

even better, Miss Kelley's book, a great part of which concerns these early stories.

28. *Letters*, i, 30–31.

29. A letter written much later contains his mature expression of his real quarrel with America. "What I mean is that here [in Europe], after a fashion, a certain part of the work of discrimination and selection and primary clearing of the ground is already done for one, in a manner that enables one to begin, for one's self, further on or higher up; whereas over there I seemed to see myself, *speaking only from my own experience*, [my italics] often beginning so 'low down,' just in that way of sifting and selecting, that all one's time went to it and one was spent before arriving at any very charming altitude" (*ibid.*, ii, 297–298).

30. Attention ought to be called to the practice, in this paper, of dating James's fiction according to its first appearance. This procedure has been adopted in order to bring the dates of publication as close as possible to the often unascertainable dates of composition, in spite of the fact that the dates given are very often those of publication in periodicals, not in book form.

31. *The Reverberator*, xx. "The first stories good enough for the collective edition were all laid in Europe" (Beach, 167). For discussion of the early stories see *Early Development of Henry James*, particularly Chapter XI.

32. See Beach, 168. Van Wyck Brooks, in analyzing James's "pilgrimage," has much

evidence on his side, but he misses the great point that the Americans whom James could best describe were people whose problems could be treated most effectively in connection with Europe.

33. *Reverberator*, xix. Another reason, which James grasped more clearly than anyone else at the time, was the virtual impossibility of there being an American novelist — there could be only sectional novelists — local-color novelists. Because he avoided the faults almost inseparable from the local-color novel, his work keeps on meaning what he wanted it to. On the American local-color novel he wisely commented, "The thousands of celebrated productions raised their monument but to the bastard vernacular of communities disinherited of the felt difference between the speech of the soil and the speech of the newspaper, and capable thereby, accordingly, of taking slang for simplicity, the composite for the quaint and the vulgar for the natural. . . . The monument was there, if one would, but was one to regret one's failure to have contributed a stone?" *Daisy Miller*, xviii–xix.

34. *Reverberator*, 320.

35. *Ibid.*, xiii; *Daisy Miller*, xix. An incident, European in origin, such as that which suggested *The Reverberator*, often cast no new light on European life, "but on the other hand, in its indirect way, flooded 'American society' with light, became on *that* side in the highest degree documentary" (*Reverberator*, xi–xii).

36. A note ought here to be made of James's tendency to be slightly more advanced in his short stories than in his novels. He always experimented in the short form first, and James's novels should then, as a rule, be coupled with somewhat earlier short stories. Thus, *A Passionate Pilgrim* and its ilk are not to be discussed along with *Watch and Ward*, of the same date, but with *Roderick Hudson*, of four years later; and *Madame de Mauves*, published before *Roderick Hudson*, is an experiment in the sort of work to be done in *The American*, which follows *Roderick Hudson*. The ideas for several of these stories were doubtless in James's mind at once, but this does not invalidate the observation that the progressive changes of approach in James's longer fiction were always foreshadowed in shorter work of a slightly earlier date. It is also true that he often kept on writing short things according to an approach that he had already abandoned in his longer fiction.

37. *The American*, xxiv.

38. *Ibid.*, xxvi.

39. See Stephen Spender, "The School of Experience in the Early Novels," *Hound & Horn*, vii (April–June, 1934), 417 ff. This article has to be taken with reservations.

40. *A Passionate Pilgrim* has many descriptions fitted for an album to be entitled "The Beauties of England"; *Roderick Hudson*, in parts, is dangerously near being a comprehensive guide-book to Rome. In both instances, the description is an integral part of

the narrative; the atmosphere causes most of the action. James was always to rely on the evocative power of physical settings, but the settings of the later books were to be just that, nothing more; they were to serve as a harmonic background for a self-contained human action, explicable in terms of personality independent from geographic location.

41. For the *raisonneur* in *A Passionate Pilgrim*, see above, end of note 23. In *Roderick Hudson* Rowland Mallet's is the evaluating consciousness, though he is not a first-person narrator. James's own later perception of the inability of the action to make itself plausible, appears in his preface to the revised novel and is illustrated by one touch in the revision, noticed by Theodora Bosanquet: "A comparable growth of ironic perception was allowed to Roderick Hudson, whose comment on Rowland's admission of his heroically silent passion for Mary Garland, 'It's like something in a novel,' was altered to: 'It's like something in a bad novel'" (*Henry James at Work*, London, 1924, p. 15).

42. Edna Kenton, "Henry James in the World," *Hound & Horn*, VII (April–June, 1934), 513.

43. *The Golden Bowl*, I, xiv.

44. "The Art of Fiction," *Partial Portraits*, 402, written in 1884. Four years later James wrote to William, "I have not the least hesitation in saying that I aspire to write in such a way that it would be impossible to an outsider to say whether I am at a given moment

an American writing about England or an Englishman writing about America (dealing as I do with both countries), and far from being ashamed of such an ambiguity I should be exceedingly proud of it, for it would be highly civilized" (*Letters*, i, 141–142).

45. *Ibid.*, i, 65–66. *The Europeans* is very entertaining light comedy, in which the differences between the New England Wentworths and their Europeanized cousins are beautifully hit off. At the end of the following year (1879), another novel, *Confidence*, began coming out in *Scribners*. Like *The Europeans*, it was meant to be light, but it succeeds in being only tediously artificial. However, everything said in the text about *The Europeans*, applies likewise to it.

46. Beach is, as ever, quite honest about *Washington Square*: "There is scarcely one of the articles in our definition of the James method which could here be applied without great modification" (*Method of Henry James*, 228). He allows it to be successful, though not distinctive. "It is anything but a good example of the method which he later made so much his own. But it is a charming memento of a phase through which he passed on the way to his more distinctive performance" (*ibid.*, 232). It is not within Beach's purpose to explain its occurrence. Van Wyck Brooks does try to explain it; in connection with it, and with *The Bostonians*, he exclaims of James: "He had known his America, he had understood it, far more deeply than he had ever supposed" (*Pil-*

grimage, 42). I cannot understand this remark, for all of James's actions, almost from the beginning, seem only too apparently to be accounted for by his exceptional understanding of his country and of his relation to it. *Washington Square* according to Brooks is an unpremeditated offshoot of a certain basically sound instinct of James's, the value of which he failed to recognize.

47. *Washington Square*, 38.

48. See *Letters*, I, 72–73.

49. *The Portrait of a Lady*, I, viii. For a parallel quotation see "Art of Fiction," 314.

50. Isabel Archer is betrayed, significantly enough, by an Italianate American, Gilbert Osmond, paired off, for contrast, against Ralph Touchett, the Anglo-American. The one is corrupt, the other frustrate; these two fates, in the Jamesian annals, exhaust the possibilities for the Europeanized American. The curse of frustration can, of course, be mitigated by the exercise of bravery and understanding. Touchett has these qualities, and Isabel's fate will, as indicated, be like his; she will make the best of a bad situation, a *best* that will principally involve attitude, only incidentally geographical location.

51. *The Princess Casamassima*, I, xii.

52. See *ibid.*, v–vii. At the end of the preface James pertinently remarked, "Let me at the same time not deny that, in answer to probable ironic reflexions on the full licence for sketchiness and vagueness and dimness taken indeed by my picture, I had to bethink myself in advance of a defence of my 'artistic

position.' Shouldn't I find it in the happy
contention that the value I wished most to
render and the effect I wished most to produce were precisely those of our not knowing,
of society's not knowing, but only guessing
and suspecting and trying to ignore, what
'goes on' irreconcilably, subversively, be-
neath the vast smug surface?"

53. *Ibid.*, xxiv.
54. *Letters*, i, 162.
55. Edmund Wilson, "The Ambiguity of Henry
James," *Hound & Horn*, vii (April–June,
1934), 402.
56. *Letters*, i, 163.
57. *Ibid.*, i, 73.
58. *Ibid.*, i, 60.
59. *Theatre and Friendship*, London, 1932, the
letters of Henry James to Elizabeth Robins,
accompanied by her introduction and narrative. James had many acquaintances connected with some branch of the theater,
among them Fanny Kemble, Lady Bell,
William Heinemann, Edward Compton,
Ellen Terry.
60. *Letters*, i, 170.
61. *Ibid.*, i, 162.
62. *Ibid.*, i, 146, in "Later London Years," one
of Lubbock's biographical sketches. There
were "seven or eight" of these plays says
Lubbock. Four of them were published, in
London, in the two series of *Theatricals*, the
first volume in 1894, the second in 1895.
63. *Ibid.*, i, 226. Even a year before, James had
written, "The whole odiousness of the thing
lies in the connection between the drama and

the theatre. The one is admirable in its interest and difficulty, the other loathesome in its conditions. If the drama could only be theoretically or hypothetically acted, the fascination resident in its all but unconquerable (circumspice!) form would be unimpaired, and one would be able to have the exquisite exercise without the horrid sacrifice" (*ibid.*, I, 211).

64. See *ibid.*, I, 227–228.

65. "You would understand better the elements of the case if you had seen the thing it followed . . . and the thing that is now succeeding at the Haymarket — the thing of Oscar Wilde's. On the basis of *their* being plays, or successes, my thing is necessarily neither" (*ibid.*, 228–229).

66. The public's disapproval of *Guy Domville* was to a great extent mitigated by the large number of private congratulations he received on his work (*ibid.*, i, 228). See, for an excellent account of the whole affair, Léon Édel, *Les Années Dramatiques*, Paris, 1931, 154 ff.

67. *Letters*, I, 229.

68. *Ibid.*, I, 231–232.

69. Édel mentions several critics who have done this, or who have preferred to ignore James's connection with the stage, and concludes with this cogent remark, "D'après Ford Madox Ford [*Joseph Conrad: A Personal Remembrance*] son théâtre aurait 'empoissoné les dernières années de sa vie,' mais, s'il échoua à la scène, ne fut-ce pas la grande habilité technique acquise en travaillant pour

elle qui fit de ses trois derniers romans ses meilleurs?" (*Les Années Dramatiques*, 235.)

70. *Theatricals, Second Series*, London, 1895, xiii.
71. *Letters*, i, Introduction, xx.
72. (1) "If the art of the drama, as a great French master of it has said, is above all the art of preparations, that is true only to a less extent of the art of the novel, and true exactly in the degree in which the art of the particular novel comes near that of the drama. The first half of a fiction insists ever on figuring to me as the stage or theatre for the second half" (*The Magic Muse*, i, xiii).

(2) "The beauty of the conception was in this approximation of the respective divisions of my form to the successive Acts of a Play. . . . The divine distinction of the act of a play . . . was, I reasoned, in its special, its guarded objectivity" (*The Awkard Age*, xix). For an excellent discussion of this see Édel, Chapter 9.

(3) Also in connection with *The Awkward Age*, James wrote in a letter, "The *form*, doubtless, of my picture is against it — a form all dramatic and scenic — of presented episodes, architecturally combined and each making a piece of the building; with no going behind, no *telling about* the figures save by their own appearance and action and with explanations reduced to the explanation of everything by all the other things *in* the picture" (*Letters*, i, 333).

(4) And again, "'Dramatise, dramatise!' — there had of course been that preliminary" (*Daisy Miller*, xxiii).

(5) Again, "The material of *The Am-bassadors*, conforming in this respect exactly to that of *The Wings of the Dove*, published just before it, is taken absolutely for the stuff of drama; so that, availing myself of the opportunity given me by this edition for some prefatory remarks on the latter work, I had mainly to make on its behalf the point of its scenic consistency. It disguises that virtue, in the oddest way in the world, by just *looking*, as we turn its pages, as little scenic as possible; but it sharply divides itself, just as the composition before us does, into the parts that prepare, that tend in fact to over-prepare, for scenes, and the parts, or otherwise into the scenes, that justify and · crown the preparation. It may definitely be said, I think, that everything in it that is not scene (not, I of course mean, complete and functional scene, treating *all* the submitted matter, as by logical start, logical turn, and logical finish) is discriminated preparation, is the fusion and synthesis of picture" (*Ambassadors*, I, xxii–xxiii).

73. Francis Fergusson, "Drama in *The Golden Bowl*," *Hound & Horn*, VII (April–June, 1934), 409.

74. *The Awkward Age*, declared James, "helps us ever so happily to see the grave distinction between substance and form in a really wrought work of art signally break down. I hold it impossible to say, before *The Awkward Age*, where one of these elements ends and the other begins: I have been unable at least myself, on re-examination, to mark

any such joint or seam, to see the two *dis-charged* offices as separate. They are separate before the fact, but the sacrament of execution indissolubly marries them, and the marriage, like any other marriage, has only to be a 'true' one for the scandal of a breach not to show" (*Awkward Age*, xxiv).

75. Joseph Conrad, *Life and Letters*, ed. G. Jean-Aubry, London, 1927, i, 271.

76. *The Spoils of Poynton*, v, vii, viii.

77. "To be at all critically, or as we have been fond of calling it, analytically, minded — over and beyond an inherent love of the general many-coloured picture of things — is to be subject to the superstition that objects and places, coherently grouped, disposed for human use and addressed to it, must have a sense of their own, a mystic meaning proper to themselves to give out: to give out, that is, to the participant at once so interested and so detached as to be moved to a report of the matter" (*The American Scene*, 273).

78. "Art is essentially selection, but it is a selection whose main care is to be typical, to be inclusive" ("Art of Fiction," 398). To R. L. Stevenson, who had written a 'Humble Remonstrance' to James's article, James replied, saying, among other things, "Excellent are your closing words, and no one can assent more than I to your proposition that all art is a simplification" (*Letters*, i, 110). See also "The New Novel," in *Notes on Novelists*, New York, 1914, particularly 326, 342 ff.

79. *Roderick Hudson*, x.

80. *Lady Barbarina*, viii.
81. See *Letters*, ii, 6, in the biographical sketch entitled "Rye."
82. See *ibid.*, i, 408–409; *Awkward Age*, v; also Bosanquet, *Henry James at Work*, 8.
83. *Letters*, i, 124.
84. See "The Ambiguity of Henry James," 394–396.
85. In connection with *The Awkward Age*, James wrote, "A work of art that one has to *explain* fails in so far, I suppose, of its mission. I suppose I must at any rate mention that I had in view a certain special social (highly 'modern' and actual) London group and type and tone, which seemed to me to *se prêter à merveille* to an ironic — lightly and simply ironic! — treatment, and that clever people at least would know who, in general, and what, one meant. But here, at least, it appears there are very few clever people!" (*Letters*, i, 333.)
86. Bosanquet, 10.
87. No more thorough misinterpretation of an observable characteristic of James's work could be made than is contained in the following remark by VanWyck Brooks: "The later James stands between ourselves and life and creates his illusion by benumbing our sense of human values" (Brooks, 145). What Brooks should have observed was that James *refused* to stand between his readers and life, refused to explain, to dictate, to make judgments, refused to give the customary artificial stimulation to our "sense of human values."

88. *Ambassadors*, i, 190.

89. As James stated in the illuminating "Project for *The Ambassadors*" (see note in Bibliography under *Hound & Horn*), "he [Strether] lingers in Paris a little — he has wanted to see the situation 'through,' but with the direction events have taken from him, it sufficiently comes over him that they *are* through. His imagination of them drops, and if he rather glosses over for the pair [Chad Newsome and Mme. de Vionnet] the quantity they have cost him, the last tribute [dissimulating his real convictions in order to help Chad out] strikes him, at last, as the very most he can manage" (p. 558).

90. James's impersonal treatment of Kate Croy contrasts favorably with Thackeray's use of Becky Sharp, whose situation has points of similarity with Kate's. James's attitude toward his characters was the sort of attitude he attributed to Balzac, one which was in direct opposition to Thackeray's. "The English writer wants to make sure, first of all, of your moral judgment; the French is willing, while it waits a little, to risk, for the sake of his subject and its interest, your spiritual salvation" (*The Question of Our Speech; The Lesson of Balzac*, Boston, 1905, 99).

91. "The subject of 'The Wings of the Dove,' or that of 'The Golden Bowl,' has not been the exhibited behaviour of certain Americans as Americans, of certain English persons as English, of certain Romans as Romans. Americans, Englishmen, Romans, are, in the

whole matter, agents or victims" (*Lady Barbarina*, vi).

92. James dropped *The Ivory Tower* because, after the outbreak of the war, he could not keep on writing about contemporary life. See *The Ivory Tower*, New York, 1917, v (introductory note by Percy Lubbock). He took up, for relief, the fantasy which became the fragmentary *Sense of the Past*, later to be adapted for the play *Berkeley Square*. He had started the story in 1900, and had given it up very quickly, since it seemed too fanciful. See *Letters*, ii, "The War," 380; also II, 426.

93. For James's reference to this remark of Benson's see *Letters*, i, 252: "I don't know, in spite of your compliment, whether I *am* much like Gray, save in the devil of a time it takes me to do a thing. What keeps me incommunicative, however, is not indifference, but almost a kind of suspense, a fear to break — by speaking — the spell of some *other* spectacle — other than that of my own *fonctionnement*."

94. *Letters*, ii, 99.

95. *Ibid.*, i, 310–311.

96. *Theatre and Friendship*, 14.

BIBLIOGRAPHY

Writings of Henry James *

Fiction

The Novels and Tales of Henry James, London,
  1920–34, 35 vols.
The Outcry, New York, 1911.
The Ivory Tower, New York, 1917.
The Sense of the Past, New York, 1917.

Drama

Theatricals, first series, London, 1894.
Theatricals, second series, London, 1895.

Miscellaneous

French Poets and Novelists, London, 1878.
Hawthorne, English Men of Letters, London,
  1879 (1887).
Partial Portraits, London, 1888.
The Question of our Speech; The Lesson of Balzac,
  Boston, 1905.
The American Scene, London, 1907.
Views and Reviews, early reviews collected and
  edited by LeRoy Phillips, Boston, 1908.
A Small Boy and Others, New York, 1913.
Notes of a Son and Brother, New York, 1914.
Notes on Novelists, New York, 1914.
Letters, selected and edited by Percy Lubbock,
  New York, 1920, 2 vols.

* For a fairly complete bibliography of the work of James see
that published by LeRoy Phillips, Boston and New York 1906.

Notes and Reviews, early reviews collected and edited by Pierre Chaignon de la Rose, Cambridge (Massachusetts) 1921.

Theatre and Friendship, letters of Henry James to Elizabeth Robins, with running comment by Miss Robins, London, 1932.

SOME CRITICISM CONCERNING HENRY JAMES

[Items which are especially worth studying are starred.]

Arvin, Newton (see under *Hound & Horn*).

*Beach, Joseph Warren, *The Method of Henry James*, New Haven, 1918.

—— "Henry James," *Cambridge History of American Literature*, New York, 1921, III, chap. VIII.

Blackmur, R. P. (see under *Hound & Horn*).

Bosanquet, Theodora, *Henry James at Work*, London, 1924.

Brooks, VanWyck, *The Pilgrimage of Henry James*, New York, 1925.

Brownell, W. C., *American Prose Masters*, New York, 1909 (1923), 286–332.

Cantwell, Robert (see under *Hound & Horn*).

*Édel, Léon, *Les Années Dramatiques*, Paris, 1931.

Edgar, Pelham, *Henry James, Man and Author*, Boston, 1927.

Fergusson, Francis (see under *Hound & Horn*).

Hays, H. R. (see under *Hound & Horn*).

Hound & Horn, VII (April–June, 1934), an entire issue devoted to criticism of Henry James, and including his recently unearthed "Project

[73]

for *The Ambassadors*," a plan for his best novel, which he sent to Harpers in the fall of 1900. The following are the purely critical articles:

> "James as a Characteristic American," Marianne Moore, 363–372.

> "Armor Against Time," Lawrence Leighton, 373–384.

> *"The Ambiguity of Henry James," Edmund Wilson, 385–406.

> "Drama in *The Golden Bowl*," Francis Fergusson, 407–413.

> "The School of Experience in the Early Novels," Stephen Spender, 417–433.

> "James and the Almighty Dollar," Newton Arvin," 434–443.

> "The Critical Prefaces," R. P. Blackmur, 444–477.

> "A Little Reality," Robert Cantwell, 494–505.

> *"Henry James in the World," Edna Kenton, 506–513.

> "James as a Satirist," H. R. Hays, 514–522.

> "A Sentimental Contribution," Glenway Wescott, 523–534.

Howells, William Dean, "Henry James, Jr.," *Century Magazine*, XXV (1882), 25–40.

*Kelley, Cornelia Pulsifer, *The Early Development of Henry James*, University of Illinois Studies in Language and Literature, 1930.

Kenton, Edna (see under *Hound & Horn*).

Leighton, Lawrence (see under *Hound & Horn*).

Lubbock, Percy, "Henry James," *Quarterly Review*, 448 (July, 1916), 60–74.

Moore, Marianne (see under *Hound & Horn*).

BIBLIOGRAPHY

Perry, Bliss, *Commemorative Tribute to Henry James*, American Academy of Arts and Letters, 1922.

*Pound, Ezra, *Instigations*, New York, 1920, 106–167.

Roberts, Morris, *Henry James's Criticism*, Cambridge (Massachusetts), 1929.

Rourke, Constance, *American Humor*, New York, 1931, 235–265.

Spender, Stephen (see under *Hound & Horn*).

VanDoren, Carl, *The American Novel*, New York, 1921 (1931), 188–221.

Wescott, Glenway (see under *Hound & Horn*).

West, Rebecca, *Henry James*, Writers of the Day, New York, 1916.

Wilson, Edmund (see under *Hound & Horn*).

ADDITIONAL REFERENCES

Conrad, Joseph, *Life and Letters*, ed. G. Jean-Aubry, London, 1927, 2 vols.

Howells, William Dean, *Literary Friends and Acquaintances*, New York, 1901.

James, Henry, *Literary Remains*, ed. William James, Boston, 1884.

Larrabee, Harold A., "The Jameses: Financier, Heretic, Philosopher," *The American Scholar*, I (1932), 401–413.

Warren, Austin, *The Elder Henry James*, New York, 1934.